This project was made possible by the Domestic Violence Prevention Fund
§ 12-29-12

Everyone Makes Mistakes: Living With My Daddy in Jail

MADISON STREMPEK

DEDICATION

Daddy, I'm dedicating my book to you.

Love,
Madison

CONTENTS

FOREWORD

"Children are the living messages we send to a time we will not see." John F. Kennedy, 35th President of the United States

One of the best things about being a kid is eating yummy food! There's so much to choose from! From tasty treats to dreamy desserts and of course frosty frozen drinks (Slurpee® anyone?)

Another great thing about being a kid is being able to share special times with your family. It could be a birthday party, holiday dinner or just hanging out in the backyard eating barbeque. No matter when, where or how much time you spend together, its being together that makes it memorable. And that's really what's at the heart of the story you're about to enjoy. Being together makes life memorable, even if separated by iron bars.

"Everyone Makes Mistakes: Living with My Daddy in Jail," is a wonderfully vivid personal story written by a kid for kids. Through the eyes of a precocious 10-year old named Madison Strempek, we ride as if tandem on a bike through some of the most poignant moments in a little girl's life that proves that the love of a child is stronger than the bars that separate them from a parent.

Awash in rich Korean-American culture and sometimes sidesplitting humor, Madison weaves a narrative tapestry that can only be described as heart-warming. From the moment she learned that her father would be going away, Maddy's is a story of sadness, hope and yes, determination that despite the physical barriers that exist between them they still walk hand in hand on this unfortunate detour along life's journey.

"I thought a person like you will never go to jail," she wrote in a letter to her father, at once capturing the innocence of a child blithely unaware that her father's life had long careened out of control because of drug addiction. "I thought jail was a place for bad people," she noted... then added succinctly, "I realized it is a consequence for people who made a mistake." Indeed, some things are so clear even a child can see them.

"Everyone Makes Mistakes: Living with My Daddy in Jail," is much more than an 'easy read' for children who've borne the high cost of families that have been torn apart by incarceration.

Yes, Madison helps kids just like her make sense of the separation, offers them hope for the future and reminds them that they are not alone in this at times cruel journey. Still, I believe the added value of her book is its potential impact on the parents who read it. In many cases, they are left to scramble, trying to pick up the pieces from the shattered lives that can accompany lengthy imprisonment. For many there will be no fairy tale ending, no redemption or reconciliation.

But for a moment they too can live the wonder of inspiration through the eyes of a child who above all loves her family... mistakes and all.

Madison Strempek's book offers many useful lessons for children who lose a parent to jail or prison. The first and most profound is the reminder that they're not alone. And that's a life lesson we can all appreciate... even when taught by a ten-year old.

Enjoy "Everyone Makes Mistakes: Living with My Daddy in Jail," as you would a rich dessert- one tasty bite at a time.

Kevin Corke, Correspondent

PREFACE

Lots of people asked me, "Why did you write your book?" I wrote my book to help kids who are going through the same (or almost the same) thing as me. Mommy and I looked, but we couldn't find books by kids for kids. There were books written by doctors and psychologists, but they don't know how I feel. So, I wanted to write this book from a kid's point of view, and help kids get through a difficult time in their life.

I felt it was important to let kids know that it's okay to love your parents even though they made a mistake. I don't want other kids to feel embarrassed that their parent is in jail. I want kids to know it's okay to talk to people about their situation..

This book is written for kids, but adults, like parents, teachers, doctors, and psychologists may find it interesting and helpful.

ACKNOWLEDGEMENTS

Thank you to all the people that helped me publish my book. Without your time and dedication I would not be able to finish my book.

Jackie Blackie	Kyler Kamp
Dawn Ciancaglini	David Larkin
Susan Clouse	Tara Luckeing
Kevin Corke	Susan Morris
Derek DePaolis	Lenelle Morse
Jodi Distad	Tina Muller
Bob Dudley	Donnie Muller
Cathy Dudley	Mary Olivier
Melissa Dudley	Lauren Rausch
Song Dudley	Gina Romeo-Venturella
Elizabeth Ellis	Helen Shields
Ragnhild Erdley	Danielle Slater
Louise Hildreth-Grasso	Jennifer Wick
	Brooke Williams

All of my closest and best friends. Life Changers 180, LLC for giving me a platform for my voice.

And most of all, my mom, Robin Strempek.

INTRODUCTION

This book shares my experience. The great thing about life is everyone's experience is different and unique. Maybe you are going through a difficult time, and someone bought you this book to help you through a difficult time. To help you through this, I left blank pages throughout the book so you can write down your thoughts, feelings, and ideas.

1

MY FAMILY

I'm Madison. I live in Maryland. I live with my mom, grandma (Mama Song), two cousins, Aunt Melissa, Uncle David, two dogs, and a cat. I have a crazy house. But if problems ever happen to me I have a lot of people to talk to. You will understand why really soon.

Mama Song is from Korea and so are my two cousins. She loves me very much, and she lets me have ice cream when my mom is not home. Sometimes she even takes me on very fun vacations. One time she bought an SUV to take me on fun vacations. We call it the "trip truck." The first vacation we went to was Disney World! We didn't even take my mom, but we took all of my aunts with us: Aunt Tina, Aunt Susan, and Aunt Melissa. I love talking to Mama Song, because she's my best friend. I can tell her anything.

Aunt Tina lives in Texas with Uncle Don Don. They have a Chihuahua named Frenchs and a chinchilla named Cornelius, but she calls him Neal for short. Aunt Tina and I make fun of Neal for pooping every time he jumps. We call him "The Poop Machine," but he's super soft. So it's okay. Aunt Tina and I love shopping together. When we go shopping we talk about all the things going on in my life.

Aunt Susan is married to my friend's dad, who is also one of my martial arts instructors. I have three new cousins who are 5, 6, and 10 years old. My cousins and I will play together and go crazy. It's a lot of fun to go to their house and play outside on the new swing set. Aunt Susan and I love to hang out and watch football. She's in the Raven's marching band.

Aunt Melissa and Uncle David live in the basement apartment. They have two dogs, Patch and Fin. Patch is a medium-size black and white dog. Fin is a big black dog. Sometimes Aunt Melissa lets me babysit the dogs. She loves taking me out with her to have fun. She likes to take me out for ice cream or walking the dogs at the park. Aunt Melissa and I spend the most time together. She helps me work out my problems. Uncle David is very serious sometimes, but he's really funny and tall. I think he's as tall as Abraham Lincoln with his hat on!

My two cousins, Julie and Jema, are from Korea and going to college here. When Julie came to America she had a very, very heavy accent. Jema's English is very good. It's fun teaching both of the cousins about American culture. One time, after church I was teaching Julie and Jema the Pledge of Allegiance. They didn't get it, because they didn't understand what the words meant and some were too hard for them to pronounce. In my head, I kept laughing and laughing about it. Still to this day, they don't get it! They've helped me learn to be patient with people that don't speak English.

Julie usually likes to play with the cat, Pepper, like me. Sometimes when Julie is home with me we play with Pepper together. But Pepper is mean. He'll hiss and swat his paws at you. But sometimes if you wake him up when he's sleeping he will go onto your lap and let you pet him. Pepper purrs so loudly when he does this. This is one of the best times to pet Pepper!

I can't forget to talk about my Pop Pop. In the summer, I always go to his house for a week and have so much fun. He takes me out to the store and lets me shop. I'm a girl and I like to shop. He's married to Cathy. I like her a lot. She's very nice and comes with me on my shopping sprees. The best little surprise in their family is Little Buddy. He's a Pomeranian. I like to call him Fluff Butt. Every time he sees me he runs in circles and jumps up on me.

My mommy helps me with anything;

martial arts, violin, homework, science projects, shopping, mini vacations, big vacations, and getting my teeth fixed. Sometimes we do "reverse dinner" and have dessert first and then eat dinner. After reverse dinner she tucks me into bed and we laugh so much it makes my side hurt. Mommy also helps me through some of the hardest times I have had in my life. She listens to me and helps me solve my problems.

My family helps me get through a lot. I think it's important to know who you can talk to when you have difficult problems. Is there someone in your family you can talk to? Family doesn't have to be your mom, dad, sisters, or brothers. Sometimes family can be a close friend.

If you don't have someone, maybe you can talk to your pet. Pets are great listeners and don't talk back. I can tell my pets everything I don't like telling humans. I left you a brainstorm page to list people you can talk to:

BRAINSTORM PAGES

Is there someone in your family you can talk to? Who?

Are there family friends you can talk to? Who?

Do you have pets that will listen? What are their names?

Are there other people in your life you can talk to?

2

THE BIG NEWS

It all happened on the Friday before Valentine's Day. I was at school having a Valentine's Day party with all my friends. Everyone brought in a treat—I brought in something called pretzel sticks. Pretzel sticks are dipped into any color chocolate. My mom and I used white, red, and pink chocolate. When the chocolate is still wet you put any kind of sprinkles you want on it. We used red, white, and pink heart sprinkles on the colored chocolate. Then we put them in a bag and tied sparkly heart ribbon around the bag. All of my friends and teachers loved them. You can find the recipe in the appendix.

After the party was over, I came home from school. I was so happy and full from my party. I did my homework and had a snack. Then Mommy came home from work at the same time she does every day. She walked in the door, and I gave her a big hug. Hours passed and it was 8:30 p.m. It was time to go to bed. I brushed my teeth and laid in bed. It was Friday night, and I usually stay up to read. But this was not the case that night.

Mommy laid on the bed with me and said, "Can we have a serious talk?"

And I always say, "Yes!" with a cute smile on my face.

Then Mommy told me the news. My smile fell to the bottom of the Earth. My eyes started to water. Then I started to cry.

3

ALL THE TALKING

Mommy told me that Daddy went to JAIL!

Whenever I'm sad, I tell Mommy to go get Aunt Melissa to come upstairs and lay with me. This time I really just wanted to be with the dogs. They always make me feel better. So, we went into the basement to see the dogs and then we talked. Patch licked away all my tears, and that's why we nicknamed him Dr. Patch. That night, we kicked Uncle David out of bed. Aunt Melissa, Patch, Fin, and I slept in bed. I tried to sleep, but Dr. Patch was difficult to sleep with. Patch kicks and stretches, and his feet tried to push me off the bed.

At about 12:00 at night I went upstairs to my bed and fell asleep. The next day I don't really remember. That was a day I had violin lessons. I didn't want to go to the lessons, because I'd just heard the news about Daddy. Mommy said it was better to keep going with our regular routine. So, we did, and the day was a blur. I can't remember how the day ended, either.

when
daddy went
to jail

I had so many questions running through my head that day. Why did this happen? How could this happen? Was it something I did? Was it my fault? Does it mean that he didn't love me anymore? Why would he do this to himself? Why would he do this to me? How can he do this to my family? Is it okay to be mad? Is it okay to cry? What will people think about me? Will I ever see him again? Will I have to move away?

On Sunday, I wrote my first letter to Daddy, because I didn't know what was going on. I wanted him to know that I was very sad, but still loved him very much.

This is the first letter I wrote to Daddy:

Sunday, February 15, 2015

Dear Daddy,

When I heard the news I couldn't stop crying. I thought a person like you will never go to jail. I know you and Mommy are divorced. She still cried anyway. So did Aunt Susan. That night I slept in the basement and had a talk with Aunt Melissa. Uncle David said that God is always with you. After he told me I started to cry again. Then I told Aunt Melissa that when I was little I thought jail was for bad people. Then she told me it was a place like a timeout. After that I realized it was a consequence for people who made a mistake.

Love,
Madison ☺

Even though Daddy is in jail, I know that everyone makes mistakes. It's taken me a long time to realize that I wasn't mad at Daddy. I was disappointed in him, because I wouldn't get to see him. I knew it was going to be hard to see him while he was in there. He'd miss all the holidays and that made me sad. Even though he is in jail, I knew he would get out soon. So there was no point in being mad. I know my Daddy loves me no matter what happens.

You might be mad at your parents at first, but if you overthink it, you will make yourself sadder. Your parents love you no matter what happens in life. If your parents do something to get themselves in jail or in really big trouble, it's not your fault. It's a consequence of their mistake. It's nothing that you did and it's nothing you can fix, but remember you're only a kid and can only do kid things. I decided to love Daddy no matter what and forgive him for missing all the special time I'd usually have with him. I knew he'd make it up to me someday.

Mommy lets me send letters to Daddy even though they're divorced. I'm glad Mommy lets me do that. If your parents don't let you send letters, then maybe you can write the letters, save them in a special place, and when they are out you can give them your special letters from the heart. Here are some questions I wrote in my journal:

Some questens I have.

Why did he go?

What does the place you go now look like?

Did you go because of work?

I left you some space to write down all of the questions in your head. Some of them may never be answered, but it's nice to write down the questions you have.

QUESTIONS PAGE

<u>MORE QUESTIONS?</u>

4

MY VIOLIN LIFE

I grew up in a musical family. My mom and Aunt Susan play the violin, Aunt Tina plays the flute, Aunt Melissa plays the cello, Pop Pop plays the guitar, and Daddy plays the trumpet. Mama Song bought me a toy violin when I was 2. When I turned 3, I got a real violin. At 5, I started to take violin lessons at Peabody Preparatory with my very British-accented teacher. Her name is Mrs. Louise. Some of her students think she's mean, but I think she is the most hilarious person on the planet.

At Peabody, I have group lessons and private lessons. A group lesson is when you play with other violinists at the same skill level as you. I have two amazing group teachers; Mrs. Morse and Dr. Lauren. They're a lot of fun and really creative. I love going to their class. We have two concerts every year, our spring and Halloween concerts. We play as a big group on stage with all different ages. On our Halloween concert, we get to dress up in our Halloween costumes. I always have a lot of fun playing all the different Halloween songs.

Mrs. Louise does private lessons with me. Private lessons are when you get to play alone, just you and your teacher. I have two solo recitals every year. I get to play a song of my choice on stage all by myself. Some people are afraid to get up on the stage and do it, but I'm not scared. Mrs. Louise and my mom prepare me to play my solo and make sure it's perfect. I remember when Daddy would come to my solo recitals and that helps me perform better.

Violin has helped me get through Daddy being in jail. Daddy plays classical trumpet and only plays for orchestras. Never in bands! If I say a title of a song, then he can hum it right away. Daddy and I both know the same songs. When he hums the song with me it always makes me very, very happy. Sometimes when Daddy calls from the jail I'll play the songs I'm working on for him. He loves it because he usually never hears me practice, so it makes him happy.

I play the violin, but maybe you don't. There are other ways to express yourself during this difficult time. Have you ever tried singing, drawing, or writing? These things really help. For example, if you like going outside and you like to draw, then you could go outside, find a quiet place, and draw. I left you some space to doodle:

<u>DOODLE SPACE</u>

MORE DOODLE SPACE!

5

CALLING MY DADDY

The first time Daddy called I heard:

This is the county jail. You are receiving a call from an inmate. This call will be recorded and monitored. Press 1 for your balance. Press 2 to add money to your account. Press 3 to stop receiving calls from this inmate. Press 0 to accept the call.

After the voice message, I press zero (0) to talk to Daddy. It doesn't matter what I'm doing. The world stops when it's time to talk to Daddy. Even if I'm busy in a class or taking a shower, I race out and answer right away. Do you know why I do that? When someone is in jail you can't call them. They can only call you.

Mommy set up a phone account for me to talk to Daddy. Even though it costs money, Mommy does it for me anyway. She knows I love my daddy very much and want to talk to him any chance I get.

I love talking to Daddy. It only happens about once a week. Whenever I miss his call, I feel really bad about it, because the line to use the phone at the jail is really, really, really long. Daddy can only call on the odd number days. For example, he can call me on the 3rd or 25th.

If you can't talk to your parent, then its always good to write them letters. These letters help you express your feelings and helps your parent find hope. The most important thing about writing letters is it lets them know you still care about them and love them very much.

Here is some space to write down some topics for your letters.

LETTER TOPICS

6

MY TEACHERS AT SCHOOL

I go to an elementary school in Maryland. I was in 4th grade when all of this happened. My school is a National Blue Ribbon School and a Green School. We have really nice teachers and all of them really care about all of their students. My 4th grade teacher is the most amazing teacher in the solar system (if you didn't know, I'm really into space!). Her name is Mrs. Olivier. I think every kid should be lucky enough to have a Mrs. Olivier in their lives. She's sweet, loving, and easy to talk to. She supported me through the most difficult five months of school.

The night of Sunday, February 15, 2015 my

Mommy told me she was sending an email to *all* my 4th grade teachers. In my head I was thinking, "Why the heck was she telling ALL my teachers this? Is it really necessary to tell ALL my teachers? How would they be helpful? Is my mom out of her MIND?!?! Apparently she is!"

I didn't want anyone to know this extremely embarrassing and sad thing about me. What would people think? Would my friends make fun of me? What do I do if other people talk about their Dad and I don't want to? What do I do? I didn't want to ever talk about it to anyone at school ever again! Ever! Why was my mom telling people at my school? I decided she must know what she's doing.

That night Mommy told me my teachers would help me if I got into a situation that I didn't want to be in. If the teachers knew what was going on, then they could help me out. She also told me she set up an appointment with Mrs. Luecking, the school counselor. I wasn't sure if I should go or not, but I agreed to meet with her.

I met up with Mrs. Luecking and talked to

her about it. I started to feel a little bit better because someone who wasn't in my family was listening to me. We came up with ideas to help me through the school day. She had the best idea ever! She let me pick from a huge drawer of journals. I got a pink one, of course. She told me I could write in it whenever I felt sad or just needed some time to myself. My teachers agreed to let me have a space in the classroom to write whenever I was really sad. In my journal, I wrote a lot of letters to Daddy. I wrote when I had free time, when I missed him, or when something good or bad happened. A lot of the things I wrote and drew in my journal are used in this book. The only difference is, my journal is covered in purple sparkly pen.

MY DAD DIARY

Today, Mrs. Luecking is my biggest supporter. Every time I pass her in the hallway she asks me about this book and how my Daddy is doing. Now that I think about it, I'm glad Mommy told Mrs. Luecking about my embarrassing and sad news. I recommend that you go to your school counselor or teachers and ask them for help.

7

DEALING WITH MY FRIENDS

At school you will probably run into a conversation or two where your friends will talk about the parent who's in jail. At first I was really, really scared. I didn't know what to do if people started talking about their Daddies. So, I told Mommy and she said to come up with a story about where Daddy was. I said we can pretend that he is on a business trip for work. I know this is a lie, but it stops people from asking private questions about my life. I'm glad Mommy and I talked about it, because it was like she gave me permission to lie. One time my friend Alex said, "Where's your Dad?"

I confidently responded, "Oh, on a business trip. I miss him a lot, but that's okay because I'll see him soon."

My school has a lot of great activities like; Muffins with Mom, Math-a-thon, School Spirit Week, Pajama Day, Health Walk, Back to School Night, Band, Orchestra, Chorus, Girls on the Run, Dance Troop, Safety, Human Relations, Harvest for Hungry, Back to School Picnic, End of Year Picnic, Field Trips, Field Day, and Donuts with Dad. I guess you could say there is a lot of great support at my school. I'm lucky to be here. But it makes me sad to participate in these activities especially when everyone's Dad comes. I still do it anyway and it makes my friends happy.

When we got into the school year, we had

this thing called Donuts with Dad. It's a breakfast set-up to eat donuts with your daddy. The school wanted to get more positive male role models into the school. So my friends started talking about how they were going to bring their daddies in for breakfast. People started to talk about how great their daddy was and that made me really sad. I almost started to cry, but I kept strong and didn't.

When I heard about this I rushed home immediately, knocked on the basement door, and told Aunt Melissa that tomorrow we had Donuts with Dads. Uncle David and Aunt Melissa told me that they would take me to Dunkin Donuts® the next morning. So we made our own name: Donuts with Melissa and David. We took a selfie and sent it to Mommy. I didn't tell Mommy, so she had no idea that we were getting fresh, yummy donuts that morning until the selfie showed up on her phone. She loved seeing me smile again.

There is another activity at school that made me feel sad. It's called Watch Dogs. Watch Dog is when your dad comes for the day and helps monitor the school. He also gets to eat lunch with you. Last year I wanted Daddy to be a Watch Dog. He couldn't because he was in jail. Whenever I thought about it, it made me really sad. I always wished that Daddy would eat lunch with me.

You should probably do what I did. If peers talk about the parent who's in jail, you should have a plan of how to respond to the situation.

One situation you might get into is when a bully says something about your parent who is in jail. The bully throws the first set of words at you. You have to throw the next set of words at the bully ten times more powerfully. You have to take the power away from the bully and show that their words do not hurt your feelings. My favorite things to say back are, "I'm sorry you feel that way," and, "Thank you for sharing." Make sure you have someone to talk to, like a teacher, and tell them how you feel.

Sometimes, it can be a friend that is being insensitive or isn't aware of your situation. Words can hurt like stubbing your toe. So in that situation, I shift the conversation and talk about the other people in my life.

Writing my book has helped me get through this, too. More kids should write books about their problems because adults don't understand us! Maybe adults could learn something from us kids, too!

Here's a page to write down things you know, but adults don't:

KID KNOWLEDGE

8

WHEN I SEE DADDY

Brenda is Daddy's girlfriend. She has two daughters, Carrie and Kelly, who are really, really, really nice. They are both older than me and in high school. They have a dog-named Rita, a Pomeranian. Carrie, Kelly, and I like to play with Rita. I like to bake with Carrie. One time Daddy helped Carrie cook some really good food. After Daddy showed Carrie how to cook, I gave her new cooking supplies.

Sometimes on the weekends I would go visit Brenda. I loved visiting her, but it felt really weird because Daddy wasn't there.

On the 2nd of July, I was with Brenda

going to the jail to surprise Daddy. I was scared and nervous about seeing Daddy, because I hadn't seen him for four months. Even though I was scared and nervous, I was just as excited about seeing Daddy. He was in a scary place, but I would be with Daddy soon. I just had to get through all the security.

The process to get in was kind of crazy, but at least I got to see my Daddy. I had to walk up to a big tall gate. Then we walked into the door and had to empty out our pockets. The weirdest thing happened after that. It felt like I was in the airport while they checked me with the hand held metal detector. After the whole "airport" scene, I took all my stuff back to a locker and sat in the back on hard, cold chairs. I waited and waited and waited.

The jail's waiting room was like a school cafeteria but worse, and no tables where you can eat. They had a vending machine with all your typical vending machine snacks and drinks. The wait was so long. The wait was like waiting for summer to start. On the website it said you can't wear leggings, flip-flops, tank tops, skirts, and a few other things (I didn't know what they were!). Some of the guards on different days of the week will let you wear things that aren't allowed, like flip-flops and leggings. That is not fair!

All of a sudden, the guard yelled my last name really loud "STREMPEK! STREMPEK!". It made me jump up out of my chair.

The guards opened the scary sliding gate. You'll never guess what happened next. Can you believe it was another airport metal detector? This time we had to take off our shoes and put them in a plastic bin. Like I said, it was just like an airport. Then we put our shoes back on and walked into a white room.

Daddy didn't know I was coming, so I went in front of Brenda and almost ran into the table that Daddy was sitting behind. My run into the table turned into a big hug with Daddy. Daddy also gave me a really big hug back. It was like a big teddy bear hug. He had the most surprised and loving face I have ever seen in my whole life.

The room we went into was very big and white. There was a staircase that led down to the jail cells. There was also a guard who sat on a tall chair and had a desk that looked over the whole room. It was like a pedestal. The guard gives the person you are seeing a ticket to tell them that their time is almost up. At the end I gave Daddy another big hug and kiss because sadly, it was time to leave. I left the place happy and almost dancing. When Mommy tells people about how happy I was she says, "Madison was so excited from seeing her Dad that she jumped on the couches all day long!"

not the
↓ Best
    Place
   to be.

Daddy in
Jail with
out me.
(Place with
no sparkle.
Place sad.)

Still
not
the
↓ Best
   Place

Daddy
in Jail
with me.
(It's sparkling
with happiness.)

I learned that you should cherish every moment you have with your family, because something bad could happen and you want to remember those happy times. Every time you see your family you should give them a big huge hug and celebrate your time with them. Whenever I see Daddy, that's what I'm going to do! What are you going to do when you see the people you love? Here is some space to write down some ideas:

<u>WHEN I SEE THE PEOPLE I LOVE, I WILL...</u>

9

TANG SOO DO LIFE

Tang Soo Do is a traditional Korean martial art. It teaches you how to kick, punch, and block. But it has taught me so much more, like respect, responsibility, confidence, never giving up, always finish what I start, commitment, strength, flexibility, and power. The dojang I train at is called Synergy Martial Arts. Dojang is another word for training hall. They are my second family. Especially my martial arts instructor Master Derek. I know almost everyone at the dojang. I have lots of friends I can talk to and help through my problems. We travel to tournaments, tests, and celebrate each other's birthdays. I know I keep saying it, but it's important to have people to talk to when you have problems.

Master Derek is the owner of Synergy Martial Arts. If Master Derek had a favorite student, it would probably be me. He helps me through a lot. We break boards and sometimes I have trouble, but he encourages me to accomplish my goals. One time I hurt my knee really badly and couldn't go to class for a while. After that, he always looked forward to seeing me.

We have belts just like every other martial art, but our belts might be a little different than what you are used to. We have 10 belts: white, yellow, orange, orange with a green stripe, green, green with one stripe, green with two stripes, red, red with one blue stripe, and red with two blue stripes. Then you wear a pre-black belt. This belt is blue and you have to take two tests to get your real black belt. Your black belt has your name and belt number on it in gold. I can't wait to get mine! Mommy already has one and her number 67101.

We have to spar. Sparring is when you fight each other with padded gear for points. I hate sparring with a passion. But Master Derek made me compete at Nationals one year. Nationals is a competition of everyone in our federation. It's a really big competition.

I competed in forms that year. I didn't place and they gave me a participation medal. I didn't like that at all. I wanted a big 1st place trophy like Mommy. After that I cried my eyes out. No one could comfort me and I wanted everyone to leave me alone. Then Mommy came over with her really, really, really, really mad face. She acted like a drill sergeant. She looked at me in the eyes with a strict martial arts face and said "Suck it up! You have one more event to compete in. You win some and you lose some. Right now you have one more chance to win. Put your loss aside, suck up the tears now, and get your game face on NOW!"

She was so mean! I wanted to cry more. I don't know what happened to me, but I was so focused on my fights. I sparred three girls with my meanest and toughest face ever. Did I tell you I hate tournament sparring? Well, I do!

A miracle happened that day! You'll never guess what I was able to do! I got 2nd place in sparring! Maybe I shouldn't hate it so much. As you get to higher and higher belts, sparring is harder, but I won 2nd place with my green belt with one stripe. Mommy said I slept with my trophy all the way home and hugged it like a teddy bear.

Tang Soo Do has taught me to finish what I start and never give up. Competing at the tournament and training in Tang Soo Do, taught me that when things are really tough in life you don't ever give up. Instead, you try harder and persevere (keep going) through the toughest things in life. In the end you will always be a champion.

What things have you struggled with in life? Maybe you struggle in school, making friends, playing a sport you love, drawing, or writing. It's okay to struggle. You have to persevere, or keep trying, until you're successful. Write down a few things you struggle with and ideas on how to improve.

<u>KEEP ON TRYING PAGE</u>

Never give up! I am a champion!

I struggle with…

Ideas to help me improve…

10

EVERYONE MAKES MISTAKES

Daddy isn't out of jail yet. I miss him and love him very much. Just because people make mistakes, it doesn't mean you take them out of your life. He's in jail for a mistake that he made. It's not my fault. It's not your fault, either. You should never blame yourself for someone else's mistakes.

I want you to remember a couple of things. Always find people you can talk to through this difficult time. I like talking to my teachers, friends, family, and my pets. Even though your heart is sad, it really helps to talk to people and pets you trust. Trust me, you will feel a lot better if you get it out.

Find a hobby that can help you work through your sadness. I play my violin, practice martial arts, and draw anime. There are so many things you can do. Find something you like to do and make it your own. Remember, we are champions.

I will continue to love my daddy and pursue my dreams. His mistakes won't stop me from being who I'm meant to be. I promise not to judge him by his mistakes, but by the size of his heart. He has a big heart. Love you, Daddy!

my love
for daddy

APPENDIX

Madison's Valentine's Day Pretzel Sticks

Yields 30 pretzel sticks
Time: 45 min

Ingredients:
30	pretzel rods
3	12oz Wilton Candy Melts (1 pink, 1 red, 1 white)
	Sprinkles (a variety of pink, red, and white)
30	Wilton pretzel bags
30	strips of pretty ribbon (pink, red, and white)

Supplies:
Wax paper
Large microwavable bowl
Fork to mix chocolate

Directions:
1. Lay wax paper on a flat surface.
2. Pour one bag of Wilton Candy Melts into a large microwaveable mixing bowl.
3. Melt chocolate according to directions on bag.
4. Dip pretzel rod into the melted chocolate.
5. Lay chocolate covered pretzel rod onto wax paper.
6. Dust the chocolate covered pretzel rod with your choice of sprinkles.
7. Repeat until all pretzel rods are covered in chocolate and sprinkles.
8. Allow chocolate to cool and harden.
9. Place chocolate covered pretzel rods into Wilton pretzel bags and tie it off with a beautiful ribbon.

ABOUT THE AUTHOR

The author, Madison Strempek, is your typical vivacious 10 year old girl; quirky and full of life. When she isn't being a 5th grader, you'll find her practicing the violin, training on the mats for Tang Soo Do, perfecting her anime drawing skills, or speaking to audiences about her inspirational story. She aspires to help people change their destiny by sharing her incredible story of perseverance, forgiveness, and love.

CPSIA information can be obtained
at www.ICGtesting.com
Printed in the USA
BVHW01s1323090218
507746BV00010B/49/P